A Little Book of Comfort

Ruth C. Ikerman

Nashville/Abingdon

A Little Book of Comfort

Copyright © 1976 by Abingdon

All rights reserved.
No part of this book may be reproduced in any manner whatsoever without written permission of the publisher except brief quotations embodied in critical articles or reviews. For information address Abingdon, Nashville, Tennessee.

Library of Congress Cataloging in Publication Data

Ikerman, Ruth C
  A little book of comfort.

  1. Consolation. 2. Bereavement. I. Title.
BV4905.2.I38   242'.4   75-34421

ISBN 0-687-22145-5

MANUFACTURED BY THE PARTHENON PRESS AT NASHVILLE, TENNESSEE, UNITED STATES OF AMERICA

*Dedicated
to the Reader
"That is, that I may be comforted together with
you by the mutual faith both of you and me."
Romans 1:12*

Preface

In nearly twenty years of writing devotional books, the question I probably have been asked most frequently by readers is this: What do you have that I can send to someone who has just lost a loved one?

Sometimes a letter would tell me that some piece in one of my books had proved of comfort, and these were the letters I came to cherish.

When readers asked why I didn't write a little book of comfort, my answer was that I did not feel qualified to offer advice on so delicate and intimate a subject.

But the years bring sorrow into each and every home, including the families of those who write devotional books. Out of such experiences the material in this book has been forged.

Here I try to share with other readers the comfort which has come to me from friends and acquaintances, and from my own spiritual struggle for strength and serenity through Bible reading and prayer.

Comfort is a two-way street—it involves the one who gives comfort, and the one who receives comfort. Therefore this book contains sugges-

A Little Book of Comfort

tions to try when offering sympathy, as well as when confronting the moments of accepting it.

Who of us can know when or where we shall be the one who gives or the one who receives? May God help each of us face individual sorrows and grow to help others through reading and using *A Little Book of Comfort*.

RUTH C. IKERMAN

Contents

1. Sorrow Changes Life 11
2. Finding the New Path 15
3. Untangle Sorrow's Problems 19
4. Do the Next Thynge 23
5. Some Suggestions for Offering Sympathy 27
6. Sift Through Your Memories 33
7. Some Things You Can Do to Comfort Yourself 37
8. Comfort's Alphabet 41
9. The Little Angel with One Wing 43
10. The Comfort in an Embrace 46
11. Solace Through Prayer 49
12. Keep on Keeping On 52
13. Courteous in Death 57
14. Sharing Life's Blessings 60
15. Strength in a Smile 64
16. The Echo of a Purr 68
17. Comforting Correspondence 71
18. Be Willing to Receive 74
19. Let Holy Scripture Comfort You 78
20. A Benediction of Comfort 79

Sorrow Changes Life

Sooner or later most of us come up against some heartache we did not expect to have to face, much less try to solve or accept and learn to live with through the remaining years of our lives.

We look in the mirror and say numbly, "I did not expect this to happen to *me*." Yet this assumption is a stupid fallacy, for surely we have seen the same thing happen to someone else.

Why do we think that death will not come closer to us? How can the cancer statistics always belong to somebody else's family? Who goes through the divorce courts if not men and women whose hearts feel the same emotions of love and hate as our own?

So perhaps the first thing which can be said about our own need to be comforted, whatever our problem may be, is that we are not alone in the situation.

Sorrow is the great leveler in this life, the one common denominator. Looking out over a large funeral gathering, a pastor friend confessed that he longs most of all to be able really to convince those who are present that each of them will

A Little Book of Comfort

sometime come up to the moment of his own death.

No one wants to admit this, even when attending the funeral of a close friend. We all think we can go on living on this earth forever, which perhaps explains why affairs are often found in such a mess when somebody else tries to straighten out the finances of the one who is gone.

We are almost afraid to be comforted, for we shrink from facing up to the reality that someday somebody else will need to be comforted because we ourselves have died and left a vacancy in the heart of someone dear.

Comfort is a universal need of mankind in this earthly life. Many are the ways which people take to find it. Sometimes that comfort seems to be only in a bottle, and the organizations fighting alcoholism find the problems of individuals multiplied after the death of a loved one.

Perhaps the comfort comes in living in the past, a form of nostalgic melancholy with so many references made to the one who is gone that friends become weary of even visiting the one who does need the comfort.

Often at times of grief we become our own worst enemies, driving away the very ones who want to help and who should be in the position to do the most to help us.

We seem to take a perverse pleasure in holding on to our sorrow, for as long as we do not take active steps to move into the tomorrows of life,

Sorrow Changes Life

then the past can stay around us as a pleasant cloak of memory.

"There is more joy in my memories than in anything I can do today without him," a grieving widow said to me. I wondered how long this attitude could last, and what would be the ultimate reality when she awakened to a world which had moved along without her.

We must fight the sense of guilt we feel when we give up our clinging to the certainties of the happy past to move forward to a more uncertain future, which may bring its own unhappiness. Now we know that if we do find happiness again it may be tinged by the fear that again this joy may be snatched from us through death.

Fears have to be faced along with the honest recognition that we are now willing to be comforted. Obvious as this statement sounds, it is no easy matter to come to the point where we will let ourselves find comfort.

There is a great abyss between life and death, and we think of the two as separated by such a great gap. But any leave-taking can be painful, whether it be the parting at death, or a separation by law, time, or distance.

The ancients had a ritual called the "waters of separation" wherein they recognized the sorrows of parting and allowed their religious leaders to take certain ritualistic steps to ease the human strain. Only after the rituals had been completed did the families feel they could go forward from the separation. In these modern days most of us must do this for ourselves.

A Little Book of Comfort

The process becomes infinitely easier if we can learn to see that death and life are intricate parts of each other. Thinking about this paradox helped me ultimately to put down in writing a bit of personal philosophy expressed here in free verse:

> My mind goes round in circles and
> Perpetually comes back to this:
> If in the midst of life is death
> Then death must be a part of life.

From this realistic assessment comes the moment when the heart can "begin to commence" to want and receive comfort. Sometimes such a moment results in a heartfelt prayer. Perhaps writing down your own prayer would lead to comfort with your individual problem. Here is a prayer from my own heart:

Dear Father, our hearts are numb and hurt, and we do not care to feel again. We would rather be spared feeling for others or ourselves, and yet we know we cannot live in this manner. To try to do so is not even to exist, and always before us is the certain promise of the "abundant life." Help us to find this again after the horror of this deep sorrow. Let us be comforted as we come to grips with what we feel about the sad ending of an episode of marriage, the loss of a friendship, or the death of one best beloved in life. Please help us learn how to let ourselves be comforted by thy grace. Amen.

Finding the New Path

Each time we come up against death, our lives are in effect changed, and we must move in another direction, find a new path. What seemed a straight course ahead must now follow curves, often with many barriers hiding the future.

We had expected to go on a trip this summer, and now we are at home taking care of all the details which follow death. Perhaps it is serious illness which is producing the sorrow, with many decisions about nursing care, paying for the medicines, when to shop for the groceries.

Always we love our own familiar routines, and sorrow first of all breaks that routine into a different pattern. We were used to stopping by a friend's house for coffee, and now we must find someone else with whom to talk or go to an impersonal restaurant, for the friend is no longer with us.

Our inner design has been moved, much as a child's set of blocks topples if the center block is jostled. None of us likes to be jostled by the forces of sorrow.

Such a nudge makes us see anew the necessity for change, and we do not want to change our habits or learn to walk a different path.

A Little Book of Comfort

Yet reason says that the longer we put off trying to walk the new path, the harder it may be to take the first steps. In such day-to-day events as shopping for groceries it is so easy to delay the matter of going to the store. If we go out of the house somebody will see us, and perhaps with the best of intentions want to talk with us about our sorrow.

It may be taking all the emotional strength we have to hang on to our emotions, and we do not want to run the risk of having to talk to someone whose natural curiosity at this time may hurt us deeply within, and even provoke a flood of tears.

It is easier to ask someone else to go get the bread and milk. For awhile friends are more than willing to do this, feeling the frustration of wanting to help and not knowing what to do for us. It is a relief for the friends to be able to do our shopping.

Inevitably the time comes when they must go back to their own daily routines. Ahead still lies the trauma of going alone to the places once often shared with the one who is now dead. Great may be the dread of going even to the store.

Courage comes to the front in life not so much in the big things, but in the little ones; so recognize that it calls for great courage to muster the strength to go to the grocery store alone for the first time.

There is more fresh sorrow in the fact that the store is still there, apparently unchanged in any way, and offering all its tempting foods, including the very ones your loved one most liked to

Finding the New Path

eat. There will of course be a stab of pain when you realize you cannot cook again his favorite recipe. Indeed you may feel guilt that you were too busy last month to bake his favorite apple pie. Now you cannot ever make it for him, and you turn your eyes away as you pass the apples, their fragrance seeming to permeate the entire store.

Perhaps it is necessary to leave the grocery store with the rest of the order unfilled, and sit for awhile in the car. Can you go back in again and finish what you started? By little steps the new path is found.

If you cannot bake the pie, now the time has come to vary your own menu, even if you don't want a new menu. You love the old one, and you don't want to try new foods. Change in eating habits or shopping habits is one of the practical problems which will have to be faced in dealing with sorrow.

Think then about ways of finding the new path in simple daily activities. Is there another way you can get to the store? Can you walk instead of driving? Can you invite a newcomer in the neighborhood to go with you? Should you consider switching to a nearer store? Can you change the day of shopping, or the time from morning to afternoon, or from afternoon to evening?

And when it comes to cooking, maybe you should drop the more complex recipes and go back to something much simpler until your strength comes back. For others, the time might

A Little Book of Comfort

be right for trying gourmet recipes in order to keep the mind stimulated and at work on something besides sorrow and memories.

The point is to keep trying to find the new path. Perhaps you might use the process which executives sometimes call brainstorming. Just write down every single thought you have about different ways of doing the old chores, without trying to criticize or reject such ideas at the time. When the list is completed, put it to one side; then go back to it a day or so later, and see which ideas appeal to you.

When you have decided which steps to try to take in forming the new path, pick out the simplest idea and get started on the procedure. Approach it in as light a spirit as possible, knowing always that you can discard the idea if it does not feel right for you after giving it an honest try. There is always another suggestion on your list which is worthy of an attempt.

TOGETHER LET US BE COMFORTED:
Father, our hearts shrink from change, and yet the old ways have been destroyed. Help us to move forward on new pathways, confident of thy presence to sustain us when the going is especially rough. Let us know that we are not alone, and that others walk their changing pathways, perhaps unknown to us. Help us to do what we can to make the way easier for others and so find our own pain lessened. Help us to find comfort in accepting change. Amen.

Untangle Sorrow's Problems

Whenever sorrow comes into any life, the regular skeins of living become tangled. Not only is the usual pattern changed and a new pathway to be found, but there are remaining snarls in the daily skeins of living.

Since these tangles happen automatically it is important to learn how to deal with sorrow's tangled threads and problems. In this regard, the advice of the woman who taught me how to knit has proved of great value.

She told me to remember, "Always let the strands fall loosely." This means to hold the yarn as loosely as possible and never to try to pull it tighter.

"When you pull hard it only makes the tangle worse," she said, as I found knots in the colorful yarn and tried to yank them out into a straight strand.

"Just let the yarn fall loosely, and if you shake it enough and let it relax, you can begin to see where you must carefully unwind the strands to get out of the tangle."

Most of us want to do as the young knitter—

A Little Book of Comfort

just pull harder on the skeins of the past and the present when sorrow enters the picture. We think it utterly impossible to relax and let the strands fall as they will, loose and relaxed.

When we learn to do this it will be possible to begin to pick up the strands and to build for the future. At the sight of a hard knot of uncertainty, we may think of a friend with a special skill who will know how to untie the problem.

Is it a financial knot? Maybe a banker will have the right word of advice, or a lawyer. So long as the individual pulls tighter on the skein and holds to the problem, the situation only gets worse.

When you relax and see what can be done to let the strand fall loosely you make room for a little clear thinking, and then you can return to the tangle refreshed in mind and heart.

If just thinking of the banker or lawyer has relaxed the problem a little, then the next thing to do is to go to the telephone and call for an appointment. If you do not know the name of the right person to call, or are in a new location, look through the telephone book for the names of organizations which help with family problems. No doubt they can refer you to the proper person in the area. Tension and strain will not solve your problem; a relaxed telephone call to someone who knows whom to call can begin to untangle the knot.

Maybe it is a matter of loneliness, which gets worse instead of better. The old contacts keep reminding you of the past, and the harder you

Untangle Sorrow's Problems

work to maintain these friendships the greater seems the distance between the past and the present. Then maybe the thing to do is to relax your hold, even on the friendships, and with a relaxed heart look where you may turn for at least temporary solace.

Is there someone lonely near you, perhaps of a different age? How about the little girl who always waves to you from the porch chair on the corner? Did you ever stop to find out whether she can walk, or does she sit there because she has a physical problem? Maybe you could read to her in the long summer afternoons. Or you may choose to volunteer for work at the nearest hospital where there is an auxiliary of volunteers.

Even before you are ready for contact with other people, there are things you can do to help as a volunteer working from your home. One way to help is by using your hands, like the one who gave me instruction in knitting.

As you learn the rhythm of knitting a scarf or a pair of bedsocks for someone else, your hands keep busy and your mind has a chance to stay in "neutral" and become quieted from the strain of the sorrow. Learn to combine the attitude of relaxing with your work on the item of handcraft, which you are making not for yourself, but for someone else.

HELP THROUGH HANDCRAFT: Take a pair of knitting needles, size 8, a skein of 4-ounce, 4-ply yarn, and cast on 150 stitches. Use the simplest known knitting stitch—just straight

A Little Book of Comfort

knit-one, where you throw the yarn over the needle and take it off with the second stitch, and proceed across the row. Turn around and come back. Three hanks of yarn will make an afghan approximately square. How welcome your hand-knitted piece will be in the home of a shut-in, or a rest home. Vary your knitting according to color, and your mood itself will begin to change if you use the gay shades. Turn the hours of sorrow into helping others, and your own heart lightens. Truly there is value in learning to use handwork in untangling sorrow's problems.

Do the Next Thynge

There is an old motto, going back to the times of our ancestors, which was often cross-stitched and framed for the wall of the home. Written in ancient script with old-time spelling, that helpful motto said

DO THE NEXT THYNGE

At any time of sorrow this is the most important single goal. Whether we feel like it or not we must do the next thing.

Sometimes friends will say, "I would do anything I could to help you, if only I knew what or how." At such times it is important to be able to tell people what to do; yet the one in shock of sorrow may not know even how to begin to compile such a list.

Therefore it is useful to remember to try to make small talk and just ask how you can help. Just say, "Do you want me to sit with you for awhile? Do you want to talk to somebody? Would you like me to keep quiet?"

One of the hardest things to do is to break the news to others who do not yet know of the

A Little Book of Comfort

sorrow, and sometime you may be asked to help do this very difficult task.

To take the news of death to someone who is not expecting to hear it calls for reserves of courage which can come only from deep inside the person, bolstered by prayers for divine guidance. It may be necessary or advisable first to telephone a doctor and make sure he is available in the event the family needs him to minister to the one to whom the shocking news is to be given.

There is no easy way to say, "He died this afternoon"; yet it has to be told before some telephone call from a stranger at the hospital, or an inquiry from the newspaper, gets to the home.

Never will I forget the dear friend in the rest home who said to me, when I went to tell her of the passing of one in our family, "My dear, how I wish I might have gone in her stead—how gladly would I take her place, if I could."

The point of course is that no one of us can take the place of another, except in some novel. In fact, this heroic substitution is what has made some novels great and enduring. But most of us know that we can take our own turn when our time comes, and not before.

Meanwhile we must be as sympathetic as we can be with others. We must expect shock on the part of those who hear the news. Most likely the response will be Oh, no! The problem is to face it as Oh, yes, it has happened.

Find out what you can do to help the person

Do the Next Thynge

accept this fact. Give the individual a chance to tell you what would be most helpful, and then both of you can know better how to proceed.

It is important to try to walk a tightrope between too much emphasis on the trivial, and getting too close to the sorrow. This is a hard balance to keep in conversation, particularly soon after sorrow.

In general, let the one who is hurt the most let you know when he is ready to talk and needs a listener. But if you are there, at least there is someone to turn to when he is ready.

Often the person bereaved is in such a state of shock he cannot drive, and your services may be useful at the wheel of the automobile.

Can you help with the telephone? Open the door to other visitors? Arrange the flowers? Provide food? Notify relatives at a distance by telegrams or letters? Just go ahead and do it, without asking for advice as to exactly how. The operator can help you locate people if you can secure an address.

Don't waste time asking endless questions and checking out details. At the time of sorrow *do something*, and hope for the pieces to fall into place. Somebody has to start putting the wheels in motion.

After details of the funeral are behind, there is the remaining temptation to push ahead on details, but now is the time to be careful not to force any issues.

Give the bereaved time to recover from the shock, but keep a watchful eye in friendliness if

A Little Book of Comfort

the period becomes prolonged without action. A friend told me how grateful she was to be "kidnapped" finally by three of her friends who came to her home one day and took her to the beach against her wishes. They said they had watched her sit inside for so long they could not bear for her not to be out in the sunshine. They took her to the beach and left her there to wiggle her toes in the sand. "Gradually I felt life returning to me," she said, "and that day in the sun marked a turning point, a new beginning."

It may not be the beach or the mountains, but any outdoor excursion can help if it is something which marks a return to life.

Sometimes such helpfulness may be needed after a friend has been involved with a traumatic experience which does not involve a death. I think of a friend who made the agonizing decision to place her mother in a rest home.

"I returned home so lonely and depressed, I thought I could not enter the house. I felt so very guilty, even though the doctor had told me this must be done. How wonderful it was to have the phone ring and hear a friend say she was coming over to get me and take me out for a ride. We just stopped for a hamburger, and didn't even try to go into a restaurant, but it was one of the best meals I ever tasted. I will always be grateful for this understanding."

Surely there is something to be done, and it is found when we try humbly to DO THE NEXT THYNGE.

Some Suggestions for Offering Sympathy

1. Try *silence* instead of talking. Just go in and put your arms around the one who has lost a loved one, and let that person know you are there. You don't have to say anything.

2. Try *flowers*. I one time came home from attending to the sad errands caused by death to find one rosebud in a blue vase on the porch by my chair. At the moment I wasn't even sure who had left it there, but the knowledge that someone cared enough to come with a blossom from her garden had in it the seeds of comfort.

3. Try *food*. One of the best discoveries I ever made about living was that it is as easy to bake two cakes at once as it is to bake just one. I have two identical angel food pans, and it only takes another five minutes to mix the second angel food cake mix, and put both full pans in the oven at once. The same system works as well with two loaf tins which hold pound cakes. Baking two identical cakes at once gives me one for our family, and a second to share with others. A slice of cake with a cup of coffee may be all the one in sorrow can possibly manage to eat for a day or

A Little Book of Comfort

two. And you can provide this comfort if you take the cake out of the freezer and leave it at the door of the home. You don't even have to go inside to see the grieving one, but can hand it to the person who answers the doorbell.

4. Try a *personal note*. If you feel up to it, sit down and write that note of sympathy right now. If you don't know what to say just enclose the clipping from the newspaper and add "I am so very sorry." The family always needs extra copies to send to relatives, or to use perhaps for information later in dealing with legal matters.

5. Try a *card*. Some commercial sympathy cards say too much and are too emotional and sentimental, but occasionally there is one which seems just right. When you find this one, buy several and keep them on hand. Then you can address one the very day you hear of the bereavement and get it into the mail *now*. Don't expect it to be acknowledged, even though current etiquette books seem to indicate that even cards should be answered with a card or note of thanks. Just get your card of sympathy into the mail immediately as the substitute for a personal handshake.

6. Try *organizing a group to help*. If you are a leader, and used to telephoning people to serve on boards or drives, now is the time for your executive ability to come to the front. Get on that telephone and call the members of your friend's club or her church circle or study group. Find out

Some Suggestions for Offering Sympathy

who will take over a meat loaf, who can provide homemade orange bread, and who has time to pick up the food and take it to the family home. A time of sorrow calls for all the strength and ability each friend possesses, and somebody has to organize such procedures—they often don't get accomplished if left to chance.

7. Try *offering your time as a consolation*. Someone may be needed to stay with an elderly relative while others go to the funeral. Particularly if the older member is in a rest home, it may prove comforting to all the family if some friend will stay home from the service itself and spend that hour just sitting with the survivor who is old and frail and in special need of friendly reassurance.

8. Try *copying a favorite Bible verse*. One who had lost a dear one within the year sent me a sheet of paper from a tablet and there in her handwriting was the Bible verse which had helped her the most. Seeing it written down in the familiar handwriting of my friend somehow gave it a poignancy it had lacked when I tried to read it in the type of my Bible. Just the gift of her handwriting offered comfort to me, as well as her testimony as to the power of the scripture in helping her.

9. Try *copying a poem*. Sometimes in your own scrapbook there may be a little poem which has meant much to you, or just a little sentence of

A Little Book of Comfort

comfort. One such came to me as photocopied by a friend, who said a minister had given it to her when her mother died. She passed it along to me, and the little anonymous poem offered new and additional comfort. If a piece has meant much to you the chances are good it will help a friend who knows you and your likes and dislikes. Don't hesitate to share your philosophy as expressed in a scrapbook poem or sentence.

10. Try giving a *book of the Psalms.* (The Psalms are available bound separately as an individual book.) Recently a friend used for the funeral of her husband a book of the Psalms I had given her many years before when her brother died, a war casualty. She requested that the scriptures be read now from this particular copy, because she had carried it with her to the hospital during her husband's long illness. She said the Psalms had comforted her for years, and especially so now, and that there was comfort even in the sight of the worn binding. The Psalms have powerful affirmations to comfort persons in the space age, even as when they were written centuries ago.

11. Try to *keep from giving advice.* The one who is in sorrow surely doesn't need any pious remarks from others, telling him how to run his life. He doesn't know where he may be living; he may not know what he is going to use for money. How can he possibly be in a position to accept your well-meant advice that he sell his home as soon as possible?

Some Suggestions for Offering Sympathy

12. Try to *keep opinions to yourself.* Just keep your mouth shut as to what should happen to the motorcycle or the book collection. There will be time for this later. Such comments at the time of sorrow only complicate the problem of the one who is suffering the initial stages of grief.

13. Try to *keep from being critical.* Of course your friend may not react as you think she should, but then she may have hidden thoughts in her heart about which you cannot possibly be aware. If you had all the facts in hand, you might understand exactly why she is acting as she is. So stop critizing before you start.

14. Try *always to be kind,* and then you will find the right words to say. A mistake made in kindness somehow does not have the repercussions of those made in self-righteousness or with an attitude of Lady Bountiful. Try to recall some kindness which has been done to you by the friend you are about to comfort, and let her know that you are just trying to say thank you for her own kindness. This releases her from an overwhelming feeling of gratitude now. Let her know she has already prepared the way for anything you do in kindness now for her and her family.

15. Try *not to forget the sorrow too soon.* Life moves along with great rapidity, and the house which has been filled with people and flowers may be exceedingly empty even a week after the death. Then is the time to remember your friend

A Little Book of Comfort

with a casserole, or by taking a jigsaw puzzle for the grandparents to try to assemble, or a cut-out book for the young children to use. It is always easier to go to make a call of condolence if there is something in your hand to talk about when the first hellos have been said.

Sift Through Your Memories

When my newly widowed friend walked toward my car on the parking lot at the shopping center I wondered just how to greet her, and ended by asking the obvious, "How are you today?"

She replied, "I'm busy sorting through my memories this summer." This gave me a chance to say, "I'm sure you have many happy memories, as do all of us."

She looked at me for a moment before saying, "I'm taking a good look at all sorts of memories this summer, before I have to go back to teaching in the fall. I want to be ready for the new season."

How wise this friend was time has proved, for she is now rising steadily in her profession and has a host of new friends from whom she probably will be choosing another husband.

She had determined to look at all the memories—good, bad, and indifferent—before moving on. This is probably what is involved in a period of grief, the true intent of the time which follows the shock of sorrow.

A Little Book of Comfort

For inevitably as the calendar turns from one month to the next it becomes necessary to "see the year through." How painful may be the first birthday alone, the first Christmas, and the first Easter! By just getting through the first year, it should be possible to feel that eventually some new year will be better than the one lived in sorrow.

Sorting through tangible possessions provides a good time to sort also through the intangible memories. Here is a lovely pink figured dress which the dear one always loved; he was especially complimentary whenever you slipped into it for a special evening.

Ahead of you is the choice of enjoying the dress and remembering the happy memories, or getting rid of it because of tears. In either event, there is time to sift through the memories and decide which will be your attitude.

By each positive choice to select the happy memory you make it easier to build a structure of happiness and replace the worn-out one of sorrow.

If you hold to the memory of the tears and clutch the dress the more tightly to yourself, you have a poor foundation on which to build for the future. Releasing it into the life of someone else may be the way to make room for some new experience to come into your life, even as it may be time to choose a lavender or blue dress instead of the pink.

Happy memories need to be shared, just as do clothes which are no longer worn or needed. This

Sift Through Your Memories

is particularly true if the memories belong to those who are in the elderly years. How will children or grandchildren know of happy picnics down by the lake, or of something funny which happened at greatgrandfather's wedding reception, unless the adult remembers the happy memory and shares it across the generation gap?

Sometimes it seems hard to recall the happy memories, harder even to speak of them than of the sad ones, but doing so has its therapeutic value. No sense of guilt should attach to telling a happy story about the one who is gone; indeed he may live again through the memory of his chuckle or deep-throated laugh at a good joke.

This is a part of the truth of the old axiom, "Let time do its healing work." Time heals only as we give it an opportunity to do so, sifting through memories, and turning them over for a fresh look.

Even as gems which have come through a fire have a special glow when sifted through the ashes, so do the memories of the past often glisten and shine when reexamined in the light of the present day.

Today's young people have such an apt phrase, "Get with it." This means get with the happy memories, and away from the sad, a doctor friend said to me in commenting on a tragedy.

It may not be easy to get with it, and our hearts as well as our hands may be involved in sifting through memory, but this is one of the

A Little Book of Comfort

tasks which grief assigns us. And the healing power of time waits to restore us to wholesome living if we expend our energies in sorting out life's many happy memories after any experience of sorrow.

Some Things You Can Do to Comfort Yourself

1. Sit down in your favorite easy chair and pick up a familiar book, or your favorite piece of handwork. Let mind and hands keep busy even as your heart tries to fathom the sorrow.

2. Listen to music. If you think you can't do this because of emotional reaction, then maybe this is the very time to turn on the record player. Just let the tears flow, and get them out of your system. Turn a radio dial, or pick up a forgotten musical instrument.

3. Look at a flower. Don't say it just reminds you of the flowers in the hospital room or beside the coffin. Look at this flower as though you had never seen a flower before—study its petals, smell its fragrance, see how it joins the stem, look at the shape of the leaves. This has the effect of getting your mind off yourself and on to some part of nature which is available to each of us. From this may come a new interest in gardening.

4. Take some physical exercise. Maybe you don't want to step out of your house—many people in sorrow find it extremely difficult even

A Little Book of Comfort

to walk to a mailbox. But go outside and walk to the corner, and drop in the envelopes with the checks for the bills which accumulate at times of sorrow. Or just walk inside your own yard around your own house, as preparation for the return eventually to life's errands in your hometown.

5. Pick up the telephone. Call someone yourself, and start picking up the strands of living. At times of sorrow, others get into the habit of calling you, but the time comes when you have to do the calling of others, reversing the flow of interest. Treat yourself to the luxury of a long-distance call to someone to whom you usually write, the sound of whose voice could have healing powers now and give you a needed lift.

6. Go out into the kitchen, and throw away the odds and ends left over from the food brought into your home at the time of sorrow. If you have not opened the special jar of orange marmalade, do so now, and spread it on a piece of toast from the leftover loaf of bread. Keep none of the special foods unopened, for they were brought to comfort you now, by people who wanted truly to help you. Use these foods for the sustenance of your body, and for special reflection on the kindness of those who tried to comfort you through food. Then start cooking with your easiest, most familiar recipe. Later you can try new ones in cooking as therapy.

Some Things You Can Do to Comfort Yourself

7. Finish those notes of thanks. Nothing is more debilitating than having them hanging over your head, and dreading writing them. Sometimes such notes prove a real mental and emotional block for the one in sorrow, even to those normally used to dealing in words. If it is beyond you to add a sentence or two of your own, just use formal printed cards and sign your name. But get them in the mail *now*. Don't expect your handwriting to look as it usually does. Even the hand itself sometimes trembles long after the onset of sorrow. Your friends will not expect perfectly phrased and beautifully written notes if they are indeed your friends. On the other hand, if it seems that you must do these in perfect style, then spend time polishing them. The important thing is to get the notes written and behind you, so you can get on with the business of living.

8. Make some simple decision about something which must be disposed of—perhaps just a book or a vase or a piece of clothing. Don't delay any longer. Make one simple decision today, and eventually the larger decisions will fall into place.

9. Make a list of things you have always wanted to do "when I have the time." Now that you have the time you may not want to do them, but it's worth a try to write the ideas down and see which one of them will spark your imagination and enthusiasm.

A Little Book of Comfort

10. Remember, your friends love you and would help if they could. There is comfort in this old Arabian proverb, sent me by one who had suffered great loss and who wrote to thank us for our efforts to try to be of comfort. In thanking us for friendship he reminded us: "A friend is one to whom one may pour out all the contents of one's heart, chaff and grain together, knowing that the gentlest of hands will take and sift it, keep what is worth keeping, and with the breath of kindness blow the rest away."

Comfort's Alphabet

Here is a little game to play as you sit in your chair and rest, trying to overcome the mood of gloom produced by your own sorrow. Make for yourself an alphabet of comfort, choosing one word for each of the letters of the alphabet. For a starter here are my own words:

A—Accept	N—Negotiate
B—Bless	O—Open
C—Consider	P—Prepare
D—Desire	Q—Question
E—Express	R—Respond
F—Find	S—Seek
G—Grow	T—Think
H—Help	U—Undertake
I—Invite	V—Volunteer
J—Join	W—Work
K—Know	X—Examine
L—Love	Y—Yield
M—Measure	Z—Zoom

Next, finish the sentence begun by the word you have chosen from your alphabet letter. Here are the first three from my list

ACCEPT sorrow's challenges.
BLESS all who are trying to help.
CONSIDER what I can do next to recover.

A Little Book of Comfort

Make each sentence something which matters to you personally, whether or not it would be meaningful for another member of your family or for one of your friends. When you have completed the alphabet, go back and select other words and make new sentences. Keeping your brain active in trying to find a solution is one good way of moving into action to solve your problems and become your own comforter. Think of the words and sentences you can make from Z—ZOOM into new happiness, ZEST for life.

The Little Angel with One Wing

Sometimes reading a short inspirational article will provide momentary comfort and start the mind on new trains of thought. Included here is a little piece of mine which appeared first in *Sunshine* magazine. It is called "The Little Angel with One Wing."*

When I first saw the little ceramic angel, she was on a sale counter near a pile of old books. The smile on the face of the little figurine was so enchanting that I moved closer, only to discover with a pang that the little angel had only one wing.

No doubt this accounted for the fact that she was with the "reduced in value" in this antique shop. She still carried a red apple in one hand and golden school books in the other, as if she were intent on learning.

So the little angel with one wing came home with me to my writing room. Sometimes when my dreams did not all turn out as expected, I looked at the smiling figure and thought how all

*Used by permission of *Sunshine* magazine, in which this story appeared in October, 1975.

A Little Book of Comfort

of us lose one wing of hope occasionally. Could I keep on as did the little angel companion?

Children automatically gravitated to the little angel, fondling her and stroking the one good wing. Always they asked, "What happened to the other wing?" Sometimes together we would make up a story about the missing wing.

She had lent the wing to another angel who had a heavy load. She forgot the wing one day when she was flying home through a snowstorm. She was saving the wing to use on a flight to the full moon through the starry sky.

One day two little girls came at once to admire the angel, and their combined delight proved too much for the little figurine. As one tried to hand her to the other, they dropped her to the floor, and there was a loud crash followed by crying.

Both of them said through their tears, "We broke the angel. Now her other wing is gone."

It was true. The little angel lay on the floor with her second wing a few feet away.

I gathered the little girls in my arms and said, "Well, neither of you is hurt, and I am so glad you told me the truth about breaking the angel."

We picked up the little figure and the wing and went in search of my husband, who turned to his tube of glue. Gently he put the wing in place, and by nightfall the angel was again smiling in her accustomed place.

My husband said, "It's too bad you didn't have the other wing, for I could have put that back on for you, too, just as easily."

But someone had long ago discarded the first

The Little Angel with One Wing

wing. Now the little angel with one wing constantly reminds me not to let go of the wings of hope.

If the first and best hope is gone from our lives, surely there is one remaining wing so life's dreams may be repaired.

So may it always be with your dreams and mine, says the little angel with one wing, smiling from her shelf with her secret store of learning.

This story has been used here to remind us that *hope* is one of the most important attributes which goes to make up the process of being comforted. So long as there is something left to hope for, life has its possibilities for happiness. And surely there is something for which you can hope today. Exactly what is it—can you determine now, this moment, from your heart?

The Comfort in an Embrace

Each summer the little girl visits her grandparents, who live near us. She comes a long distance from across the sea.

Last year she was so timid and shy she would hardly speak even to say "hello" or "thank you." She would only nod her head if you asked her a question which could be answered by "yes" or "no." Shyly she would turn her face away from you while she said her soft replies.

This year as summer approached I looked up from the kitchen where I was preparing supper, and saw a little girl walking toward the house with the little girl of our neighborhood.

They paused at the top of the driveway as if talking over whether to come down. Then they came skipping down the pavement, breaking into a run as they got closer to the porch. I opened the door and stepped out, and they came bounding to me.

The little girl from afar had her arms wide open and came over and hugged me tight around the knees. I stooped down to put my arms around her, a moment of such unexpected and overwhelming love that I felt comforted for grief

The Comfort in an Embrace

which had occurred in the intervening year since her visit.

As she pulled away from me the little girl said, "We're back. We sleep a whole half night away from here." Her tongue was loosened, and she wanted to tell me all about the last year.

On and on she talked, telling me about her school, her puppy, what she had to eat on the plane, and asking if she could come inside "the room," which is what she calls the place where I have my typewriter and books.

I wondered what had happened to her in the year she had been gone. What inner changes made her now speak so openly? Was it the power of the love which she had somehow felt when with us, but had not fully accepted when younger?

Now she was freely talking to me, and came over again to give me a warm embrace. There was comfort in her arms around me.

For some reason my adult heart had been like that of the little girl, shy and afraid to speak of the things which had happened and which had hurt.

Something in the moment of embrace released some of the pent-up emotions and longing, even as love had loosened her tongue until she was no longer afraid to tell me of her life.

Couldn't I trust God's love enough to loosen my fears and griefs into his keeping? Perhaps I could talk out the need for comfort, secure in the friendly embrace of compassion.

A Little Book of Comfort

All of us need the touch of sympathy in our lives at one time or another. Since the little girl spontaneously gave me the solace of her embrace, I have not feared to embrace others with my arms and in my heart.

Solace Through Prayer

A young father of our acquaintance has been working hard at his daily job and at home taking care of his small son and daughter, following the unexpected departure of his attractive wife, resulting in divorce.

As is often the case, one party wanted the divorce more than the other, and his sorrow was compounded by the fact that he lacked confidence at first in caring for the children.

Some of his older friends tried to help by providing an occasional supper dish or a birthday cake. Gradually a new schedule developed, and the abbreviated family seemed to be having fun together and moving into better days ahead.

Relaxing after a swim, the father told me in a revealing moment the secret of his newfound poise: "Believe it or not, I am learning how to pray."

He said it was the children who first revived his interest in something he had long overlooked. "They said their nightly prayers about lots of things, as their grandmother had taught them."

One night when the father was just half listening in fatigue and boredom, the small son

A Little Book of Comfort

turned to him and said, "Daddy, tonight you can have most of my prayer—I don't need it all just now, so you can use it."

The father was shocked at his son's perception, for he had indeed been depressed, and wondering where to turn next. "There was something in the impulsive way he offered me prayer time, and his enthusiasm, which got right to me," the young man said.

So he had asked himself, "What have I got to lose?" and for the first time in years had tried to pray "until eventually I seem to be getting the hang of it."

This father was proof again that prayer is a form of comfort which is available as solace in all situations. Sorrow is not always confined to death. Perhaps a family is grieving for a son involved with drugs, or a daughter who has run away from home and does not write to her parents.

Who knows the power of quiet intercessory prayer to ultimately change hearts and restore contact? And prayer is available to all ages, from the small children to the oldest and loneliest persons in rest homes.

Two emotions frequently block the flow of prayer, and these handicaps are bitterness and remorse. Both emotions frequently are present in any form of sorrow—bitterness that the event had to happen, and remorse for actions not taken in better days.

Instead life has changed now through death or divorce, and we feel normal negative emotions.

Solace Through Prayer

Then is the time just to pray on in spite of these feelings until strength and solace come through the healing power and blessing of prayer.

Here is a simple one-sentence prayer to use as a starting point:

Dear God, forgive us for the mistakes of the past, the resentment of the present, and prepare us for better service in the future. Amen.

Keep on Keeping On

A friend who for many years had taken care of a mentally retarded daughter told me once that her very favorite Bible verse was the portion of John 13:1 referring to Jesus, who, "having loved his own which were in the world, . . . loved them to the end."

It is so easy to love for a little while, and often so very hard to love to the very end. Yet if our comfort is to be enduring it must keep on keeping on, for as long as the individual needs our help.

So many things happen in life to change our degree of love—the trivialities, the criticisms, the constant fault-finding, the daily weariness of meals.

How true that had been of my friend whose child could not learn to play as did her playmates, much less learn with them in school. Think of the discouragement as she watched the others outstrip her own beloved daughter, even in the simple childhood games.

Yet my friend always seemed patient and loving and kind. How much strength and

Keep on Keeping On

courage it took to overcome the daily discouragement which must have been hers none of us could know.

Through good years and bad, she loved the girl and kept her neat and clean, feeding her and washing her bibs after the tedious trial of each feeding.

She loved her to the very end, and great also was her need for comfort when the girl was removed from her earthly presence. Yet by the way she had handled her own problem, she had furnished great comfort to many of us along our own daily pathways, far different from that of my friend.

You may not see how you can possibly take the long road with your own sorrow and stay with your grief until you work through to the other side. There may be days when it seems that the situation has no ending, that it will just go on forever.

Then is the time to ask "So what if it does?" Our commitment in life is to two goals:

    To see problems through to the end.

    To love during all that time.

Therefore it is possible to learn to comfort others by remembering just to love them to the end. Meanwhile we have a daily choice in the degree of cheerfulness with which we face a burden of sorrow.

The time can be spent in complaining or put to good use. One of my friends was most faithful in visiting her dear mother in a rest home, year

A Little Book of Comfort

after year. She went each day, taking with her some handwork.

One morning she came to pay a condolence call in our home, bringing with her a gift package in white tissue. Inside was a string of white beads crocheted on thread into a long necklace. The card said, "I have enjoyed the time spent making these for you. With love," and she had signed her name.

Every time I put on this necklace I recall the lovely moment of the gift, for I knew my friend had spent the hours at her mother's bedside crocheting this necklace. In an hour's time the string grew much less than an inch on this delicate work, and here was a long double strand to contrast with a long blue dress.

Always I am comforted and happier when I wear the necklace. For this friend had spent time on a gift for me, and had given it to me at a time when I needed comfort. But it would not have been available if she had spent her own hours at the bedside in self-pity or depression.

Instead she had blessed her mother with her presence, and had made an outreach toward others by her handwork, which proved a beautiful gift to me at a time when beauty was a comfort to the heart and eye.

This friend was trying to show me that she cared, and isn't this the essence of what comfort is all about? Simplicity and beauty had been woven into a chain of friendship by a friend who cared and who could not know how much her gift would mean.

Keep on Keeping On

Most of us never know when we comfort others the best. In my hometown church there is a young mother who managed to make it to church on the Sunday between the death of her husband and his funeral on Monday.

She told me that this particular day happened to be the birthday of her little girl, who wanted to come to Sunday school; and the mother said, "I thought the least I could do was to see that she got here, if it would be of any comfort to her."

The little girl spent that Sunday morning with her favorite teacher and classmates, while the mother sat in church alone in the family pew. She sat erect with her head high unless bowed in prayer, a great tribute to her faith in God, in spite of her personal sorrow.

Little did she know that just by keeping on keeping on she was helping others who had battles to fight and sorrows to put behind them, who had come to the church that morning.

Our actions in going forward at a time of sorrow may prove of inestimable value to neighbors and friends and onlookers in ways of which we have no real knowledge.

Only by going forward can you move away from the past and the sorrows of the present. Momentum once lost is hard to regain, so there is power in keeping on with simple tasks.

We are a part of one another in this lifetime, and this is never more true than at a time of sorrow. As we keep on we discover that grief is like a great kaleidoscope—the toy that children use which arranges and rearranges various components in an infinite variety of patterns. Life's new pattern emerges as we keep on keeping on.

Dear God, we need thy loving presence with us, if we are to keep on keeping on. Help us day by day to do what lies nearest at hand, trusting thee to give us patience to endure to the end. Amen.

Courteous in Death

Usually there are so many business problems following the death of any adult that sorrow is compounded by confusion. It is normal to dread facing details in advance; yet to avoid them in the last analysis constitutes a form of rudeness.

Here is a little vignette which tells the story of a man of integrity who managed also to be

COURTEOUS IN DEATH

Serving as active pallbearers were the officers of his service club. Behind them sat the honorary pallbearers, esteemed colleagues in his profession.

Beside the blanketed casket were immense floral pieces bearing the insignia of fraternal orders to whose charitable activities he had given much time and energy.

Two ministers were conducting the funeral services, speaking of his loyalty to employers, his fidelity as a family man, his understanding of friendship.

Inside the intimate, private mourning room sat his widow, whose composure had been a marvel

A Little Book of Comfort

to all her friends. One of her sons has told me the precious secret of this poise.

It seemed that when the family had gone to the bank to make necessary financial arrangements following his sudden death by automobile accident, the banker had said, "There are no problems. All the financial details are in order."

A telephone call to his attorney had brought the message: "Tell her not to worry about a thing. His legal affairs have been taken care of regularly."

The family was escaping the mad scramble which many widows of busy men face when they are stricken on the golf course or lost in an airplane crash.

What had he done to make the lonely tasks easier? He had followed a few simple steps which any man may take in any community, large or small.

He had consulted with his banker as to what were the federal and state laws concerning estates and had made sure his accounts were in line with such rulings. Signature cards had been signed and were on file.

His investments had been listed for his lawyer on a sheet which gave details about his social security number and insurance policies.

And he had taken time out from all his business duties to make an appointment with his lawyer to draw up a simple but adequate will, which had been updated as circumstances changed. His lawyer and his family knew where to lay hands on the signed copy and duplicate.

Courteous in Death

Beyond these businesslike details he had added a characteristic gesture of generosity which will serve as an eternal reminder of the high caliber of his thoughtfulness.

It developed that he had given his lawyer a plain envelope to be handed to his widow. Inside was a notecard such as those used by after-dinner speakers.

Scrawled on it in the bold, angular handwriting by which his friends had identified his Christmas cards was one sentence for his widow.

This card said: "My dear, I have every confidence that you are meeting this situation with the same spirit which blessed my happy days with you."

Long after the service the card remains her most cherished legacy. Remembering it, I think of all the praise lavished in the eulogies about his public service.

The speakers did not know of the most important tribute of all. For here was a man who remembered to be courteous in death.

TIME TO PREPARE IS NOW. What can you yourself do to make sure that others are not treated rudely at the end of your life? A few simple steps can assure courteous treatment to your loved ones at a time when they need all the courage and help they can receive. Your present action can prepare the way for the giving of great comfort.

Sharing Life's Blessings

A widower said to me recently, "I never knew how many causes my wife helped until now that she is gone and I am trying to sort out her mail."

He told me also with a wistful smile that he was surprised that he was finding a real measure of comfort in learning to support the organizations which had been of interest to her.

"She took care of all such financial donations for us," he told me, "as I was busy making the living. She wrote the checks and took the lists to our income tax man, and I trusted her judgment."

Now he found that there were personal letters of appreciation coming to him as well as the routine formal requests for funds. They were in effect an extension of the outgoing personality of his wife, and he was comforted to know that others joined him in his loss.

Especially did he prize a letter from a young medical student, who said that the wife had learned of his need for a special textbook and had provided funds for it. The young man wrote: "She shared life's blessings." And he had added a word of real comfort to the widower: "I count

Sharing Life's Blessings

you as one of my blessings, even though we have never met."

That remark had comforted my lonely friend, and it had done something else of importance for his life. The letter had sparked his interest in setting up a list of gifts based on his own native interests.

These gifts could not be large because of the expense of long, continued illness, but he had realized that at least he could do something, and had proceeded to do so.

"I found out that there are special camps for blind children, and that there are even magazines for them," he told me.

He had sent for a copy of a magazine in Braille and been intrigued by the new system of mechanical printing, speeding up the formerly laborious hand system of punching out letters.

From an appeal which came to the house he discovered that there is a special organization designed to help prevent suicide and to assist the families of suicide victims. "My wife had been sending a little check for years to their summer camp fund to help children who had lost a parent by suicide."

It gave him satisfaction now when he signed a similar check and sent it on its way to a national suicide prevention organization. For the moment this took his mind from his own loss.

He confessed to me, "We were so happy, I just took it for granted other families were, too." Reading the literature from organizations designed to help with problems had enlarged his

A Little Book of Comfort

own vision of what he might do to be useful.

It had come as a relief to him to locate an organization which would even help dispose of the personal possessions of his wife through a well organized thrift shop.

"They sent in such nice volunteers to pack clothing and jewelry, and disposed of it in a dignified manner. I was so glad to learn that her nice things truly helped provide funds for cancer research."

He was investigating ways of setting up his own will so that his possessions would not be disposed of in an estate sale or garage sale, but dispensed through a worthy organization.

"Learning about all the needs in the world somehow helps make my own grief less," he told me; "but sometimes still I am so lonely I think I can't stand it."

The next step for him probably is serving in some volunteer organization where he meets people. He may want to take his place on one of the boards and give of his business expertise, but there are also opportunities to work directly with children as a foster grandparent, or with the aged ill.

As he finds his place of service in some organization there will be new companionship based on shared interests. Truly there is wisdom in sharing life's material blessings and native talents.

PROJECT: Do you really know what your interests are? Do they lie with helping the blind, the

Sharing Life's Blessings

deaf, the aged, or children? Do you like to work with your hands or outdoors? What your real "ruthers" are can be very important to know, for therein lies tangible comfort as you share life's blessings.

Strength in a Smile

Striding down the hallway of a convalescent home, I almost passed the room before I noticed a patient smiling from the bed by the window.

Something in the smile stopped my walk, and I turned back. The face on the pillow belonged to a woman with whom I had shared responsibilities on church and community boards in earlier years.

So I entered the room and said, "I didn't know you were here, but I recognized your nice smile."

She took my hand and said, "Thank you, thank you; that is the nicest thing to be said to me in months. I am trying to keep on smiling—it's just about the only thing left that I can try to do. You don't know how much your words mean to me, and that you knew my smile."

She had reached the stage in life where to smile took much extra effort, and she was extending it day by day, hour by hour, minute by minute. Her smile was doing double service, for it had attracted me to her bedside, and reminded me forcefully of the comfort in a simple smile.

Strength in a Smile

Wisely my friend recognized that there is strength in a smile, whether it comes from the patient or the one who is in attendance at the nursing home. Certainly it cheers the visitors.

Now we chatted for a few minutes about some of the projects on which we had worked. She asked me if I remembered "the tons of fresh fruit salad" we had made for luncheons.

This reminded us of the benefit cookbook with all the delicious recipes from wonderful cooks. Our brief visit ended, and she said, "Please come again—I'll try to have a smile for you."

And she always did, for as long as she occupied that bed. If I was in a hurry I would step to the door and we would simply smile at each other and wave, and I always went on my way refreshed.

What a simple thing is a smile, and yet it means so much. There is strength in a smile, even as there is power in silence. Too much energy is often wasted in talk and in scowling and frowning.

The psychiatrists say that if you can just get a sorrowing patient to start to change his facial expression you may be at the beginning of psychic recovery.

Even a tiny smile will indicate that the problem is beginning to seem smaller in magnitude. The breakthrough to recovery often comes when the patient can give an audible laugh, even if it is a rueful one of neglect or regret.

A Little Book of Comfort

Sometimes emotions of grief are so great that words cannot escape through the lips. This is the time to try to force the lips upward into a smile, even if there are tears in the eyes.

Admittedly, smiling may take quite a little doing in certain circumstances, but as in any art practice makes perfect. The strength in a smile makes it possible eventually for the one who is in deep grief to shoulder daily burdens more easily. Meanwhile it certainly makes life more bearable for those who are trying to help solve the problems.

Even as the smile attracted many friends into the room at the convalescent home, it helped to keep the patient thinking of better days as visitors were led to talk about happy events of the past.

Ultimately a smile leads all the way back to childhood, for babies have the art of switching from tears to smiles almost in the same instant. This is a part of their charm. In the midst of loud wailing and crying, if something else attracts their attention, they will instantly flash a smile, even while the tears are still on their faces.

Then a mother can wipe away the tears and enjoy the baby's smile. How much joy is added to life when those in sorrow try bravely to smile on anyway, hiding their pain, and searching for something new to take their attention.

A LESSON TO PRACTICE: Take out a hand mirror and put it before your face. Take a good

Strength in a Smile

look at your face in its natural pose. How hard is it for you to smile now? Do you think you have forgotten how as a result of life's hard blows? Then practice in private until you can flash a smile in public, for a smile has both comfort and strength.

The Echo of a Purr

Happily the little girl put her kitten up against my ear and said, "Listen, purr-purr." She crooned the phrase over and over so loudly that I could hardly hear her kitten as it purred obbligato to the little girl's chorus.

Within a week the child was back on my doorstep crying as if her heart would break. The little ball of white fur had darted in front of an automobile.

I gathered the little girl into my arms and told her how glad I was that she had not followed the kitten, but that she had stayed safe on the sidewalk and had not been hurt.

What else could I say to try to comfort her? Nothing, I decided, and let her cry. She said her mother said she could come over and tell me about it, and this I took to be a compliment.

For I remembered back to when I had been small and a neighbor had teased me for a long time because I was lonesome for the stray cat which had mysteriously disappeared.

Who are we as adults to think we can make fun of the grief of a child? Even now as I sat with the little girl I recalled how lost I had felt when the

The Echo of a Purr

cat no longer appeared at our back door for handouts.

Far better to let the little girl cry her heart out now because the kitten had been killed than to have her sorrow go "underground" only to arise in later situations as blocked emotion. Such happenings can come back to haunt adults when they must face greater grief.

What could I do now to help her orient her grief? Taking her by the hand, I led her into the writing room in search of something to distract her attention. Near the doorway on the blue rug is a huge pink shell from a happy trip to a foreign beach.

On an impulse I picked up the shell and placed it to my ear. Yes, imbedded deep within it was the sound of the rushing water, a fascinating phenomenom which has intrigued me since I was a child.

Telling the little girl to be very still, I sat down with her on the floor and held the shell to her ear. Wide-eyed with wonder, she listened in rapt attention, momentarily forgetting the white kitten.

I searched for words to tell her what was in my heart. For the water which had rushed over the shell obviously was not in the room with us, and yet some vestige of the experience remained within the shell.

Even so the kitten would not be in the room with us to play with a ball of yarn, but some part of the kitten remained with us as we heard the echo of a purr.

A Little Book of Comfort

When at last the little girl put down the pink shell I said to her, "Honey, let us listen close and see if we can hear the purr inside," and I pointed to my heart.

She put her little hands on her fat tummy and raised them up toward her heart, and cocked her head on one side. I was not sure that she heard a purr at first, but then she began to smile.

She dropped her hands to her side and whispered, "I go home now and tell Mommy." Watching her happy figure as she skipped away, I wished that adults had similar ability to adjust to the sounds of sorrow.

For sounds have haunting power at any time of grief. Learning to live with sounds which remind us of a lost loved one is one of the hardest parts of adjusting to grief and loss.

It may be just the call of a train whistle, which may be a problem even in normal times as it gives its restless call to new horizons. There is something in the heart which longs for the familiar and at the same time feels the tug of the unknown, and this is accentuated at times of grief.

The little girl who cried for the sound of purr-purr knew authentic pangs of grief. Her recovery began when she stored carefully in her heart the happy echo of a purr.

Comforting Correspondence

A lovely pink rosebush blooms profusely in our garden, attracting passing butterflies and birds. We cherish the fragrant roses for another reason—because the bush is a memorial gift from the brother of a friend with whom we had carried on comforting correspondence.

The card with the rose tree said: "I found the box in which my sister had saved all the cards you sent her. There was a note asking me to see that the pictures on them went to a nursery school to be used for scrapbooks, and this I did. Hope the roses will remind you of us both."

Simple correspondence is one of the tangible ways of bringing comfort, for "postal therapy" can be of great help in sustaining the life interest of shut-ins, for one with a terminal illness, or for those in the shock of accidental death.

Learning to write such notes can offer comfort to the mind involved with sorrow of its own. Two problems need to be overcome—the matter of finding time to write, and the money for materials and postage.

The time problem is solved when the notes are written at a stated period each week, perhaps while listening to a thirty-minute musical pro-

A Little Book of Comfort

gram on radio, or with the background of a light television series.

The cost can be minimized by watching for notepaper sales at inventory time; using postcards, which call for less postage; or recycling cards which come into your home.

Cut out the inner writing and save the picture. Just write your note on the back of it and place this in a stamped envelope. Children especially love such cards, even if they have no fold, for the one-sheet card can be pasted into a scrapbook.

Recently I saw a number of such cards taped to a refrigerator door by a young mother whose little daughter watches for the mail and prizes her "pictures." She gets to look at them while she helps Mommy in the kitchen, and she "writes" to us with crayon scrawls.

Even adult notes do not need to be long. Here are two sample sentences, which can be used on identical cards in any one week: "May this be a week of better health for you," or "We hold you in our sustaining prayers for recovery."

Use the same card for all in the same week—a simple card with a picture of a sailboat, puppy, sunset, or flower. It is surprising what such duplication can do to help save energy.

A card without a verse is useful in so many instances, particularly where there is terminal illness or death. The message can be written in longhand in a few heartfelt words: "We send our best to you and all those dear to your heart."

Sometimes there is hesitancy over sending a card in an awkward situation but who needs a

Comforting Correspondence

card more than someone to whom there is nothing to say? Don't try to say anything, except for your simple sentence and signature. Let those involved in the turmoil know of your loving concern.

Sometimes in long-range illness, a picture postcard of the community will take the outside into the sickroom. A picture of the college campus or the new library tells its own story to the one who cannot be there in person.

An envelope will hold a folded church bulletin on which you can scrawl the word "Hello." The same is true of a musical program or cast list from a theater production.

Using such cast-off items for notepaper proves a good way to keep in touch with older friends who have moved away, and who often long for old times and familiar scenes. Notes to us from young friends involved in military service bring special thanks for such reminders.

Shut-ins find their life interest renewed through receiving cards, as mail call is an emotional time of day. It is easy to become discouraged if friends forget, and there is generating energy in the sight of well loved handwriting on an envelope.

It is also true that once the first efforts are made to begin to send notes again after a period of personal sorrow, the way opens for receipt of happier correspondence. There is value in remembering comforting correspondence as a tool to use in recovery from sadness.

Be Willing to Receive

At the reunion her classmates were discussing one who had died during the year after a long illness. "She was always so willing to receive whatever we tried to give her."

And this had not been easy for the one in question, for she had said in her healthy years, "My independence is my most prized possession."

Little by little every bit of her independence had been taken from her, except for an independent spirit. She became helpless in body, unable to turn over in bed, needing help with her feeding.

Yet she learned to receive the ministrations of others. One friend had stopped by to comb her hair and apply her makeup. Another would arrange flowers by the bedside. The husband of a third admitted he liked to read the newspaper to her whenever possible.

This woman kept her friendships intact to the end. She did this largely by training herself to be willing to receive what others wanted to give.

In this she was in great contrast to many who stand in need of comfort, but who add to the

Be Willing to Receive

problems of others by refusing to accept what they offer with good intentions.

One of the hardest lessons life teaches is that we must be willing to receive before another can give. There is no more real and lasting sorrow than the gift refused or rejected, particularly where love is involved.

By receiving whatever is offered in a loving gesture we can learn to comfort ourselves, and prepare the way for others who may need to be comforted.

Sometimes it is a self-reliant member of the family, who must learn how to accept in behalf of loved ones. Such was the case with the husband of a professional friend. She was stricken with a disabling illness, requiring years of care.

The husband could provide financially, but he discovered there were other things which could only be provided through the loving interest of the friends of his wife. They used their business and executive experience to organize groups to run errands and make telephone calls.

At first the husband seemed to resist such attempts at friendliness, but gradually he became aware of how important it was to his helpless wife to know that her friends still cared. He learned how to make the friends welcome, and in this process made many new friends of his own from his wife's circle of associates.

When she was gone, the widower called the president of the professional group and offered the women the collection of colored glass vases,

A Little Book of Comfort

collected in foreign travel, which had graced the windows of the home.

He wanted the vases distributed among the women who had provided gifts of loving concern, which he had received in the name of his beloved wife. Into our home came a blue glass vase in the shape of a basket, just right for seasonal bouquets from the garden.

Seeing the basket on my desk one day the widower said: "I'm so glad to see the daffodils in this basket. It makes me feel good to think you keep the basket full of flowers."

It was a moment when we both understood he was saying that life itself is empty unless we allow it to be filled with the kind gestures of those who wish to comfort us in our sorrow.

Sometimes in this changing life span, we must be on the receiving end of comfort in ways not expected. Perhaps we have often given aid, but thought we would not need it for ourselves. Maybe we learn that we need a different kind of comfort than we have known before, and must welcome it from various sources.

As we learn to accept the little courtesies of our friends, we prepare the way for the acceptance of the healing which comes from God's great gift of time, and the ultimate restoration of happy memories to bless future living.

WHEN IN NEED OF COMFORT, LET US BE WILLING TO RECEIVE
Dear heavenly Father, we are grateful for the ways in which thou dost show us comfort, through the use

Be Willing to Receive

of friends and experiences in our daily lives. Forgive us our frequent failures to receive such gestures in cheerful fashion. Help us to recognize the loving intent and to receive generously, so that, in whatever circumstances, we may come to know the joy of life abundant. Amen.

Let Holy Scripture Comfort You

A letter from a friend said: "I was so very sorry to learn of your great loss. This is a situation for which there are no human words, and this is what makes the Scriptures so meaningful."

This understanding note led me to re-read many helpful verses. Each of us needs to discover our own favorite passages. Pick up the Bible and see what is the message for your heart this very day. And when you close the pages it is time to go out into the world nearest you to walk again with family and friends who have their own sorrows. Together let us be comforted:

Let not your heart be troubled: ye believe in God, believe also in me. In my Father's house are many mansions: if it were not so, I would have told you. I go to prepare a place for you. And if I go and prepare a place for you, I will come again, and receive you unto myself; that where I am, there ye may be also. (John 14:1-3)

A Benediction of Comfort

Grace be to you and peace from God our Father, and from the Lord Jesus Christ.

Blessed be God, even the Father of our Lord Jesus Christ, the Father of mercies, and the God of all comfort;

Who comforteth us in all our tribulation, that we may be able to comfort them which are in any trouble, by the comfort wherewith we ourselves are comforted of God.

(II Corinthians 1:2, 3, 4)